Dean Martin & Jerry Lewis: America's Favorite 1950s Comedy Team

By Charles River Editors

Martin and Lewis on *The Colgate Comedy Hour* in 1955.

About Charles River Editors

Charles River Editors provides superior editing and original writing services across the digital publishing industry, with the expertise to create digital content for publishers across a vast range of subject matter. In addition to providing original digital content for third party publishers, we also republish civilization's greatest literary works, bringing them to new generations of readers via ebooks.

Introduction

Dean Martin (1917-1995)

"If people want to think I get drunk and stay out all night, let 'em. That's how I got here, you know." – Dean Martin

Like Frank Sinatra, Dean Martin is an American legend for his longevity and success across a garden variety of different platforms. Martin began as a nightclub singer, performed in a comedy act, starred in films, recorded hit albums, and capped his career by serving as a television host. In fact, there may be no star who was better able to transcend the different avenues of entertainment.

Martin's success was made all the more amazing by the fact that he never had to change his personality or persona to find success in his different endeavors. From the beginning, Martin's public persona remained largely unchanged. He grew more famous and wealthy, but he always remained the smooth-talking Italian with the easy charm and the cool veneer. As Jerry Lewis noted in his memoirs about Martin, "Dean had this uncanny way of making everything bad look like it wasn't all that bad." If anything, Martin suggested that no matter the circumstances, people can always face their situation with leisurely charm.

Martin's versatility is unprecedented even today, an era in which stars routinely alternate between film and musical careers. Martin was able to simultaneously work across different media at the same time; even after rising to fame as a singer, he continued to perform with Jerry Lewis and star in films. But after his film career took off, he continued to perform the crooning style of music that had made him famous and had long since been outdated. While other actors were forced to drastically alter their persona to keep up with the times, Martin's ability to fuse suave glamour with an everyday ordinariness ensured he didn't need to transform anything.

Martin's life and career are often compared to his close friend and contemporary Frank Sinatra, and for good reason. Both came from proud Italian families, both were cohorts in the famed Rat Pack in the 1960s, and they each maintained success even late in their careers. However, Sinatra's career was filled with far more ups and downs than Martin, and his public image experienced highs and lows along with it. It's also somewhat ironic that it was Martin who Anglicized his name but remained a bigger Italian icon than Sinatra. They each began their careers as Italian crooners, but Martin maintained his style while Sinatra adopted a brasher, more "All-American" singing method. Martin never strayed far from his humble background, even as he became one of America's biggest stars.

Dean Martin and Jerry Lewis profiles the life and career of one of America's most famous performers. Along with pictures of important people, places, and events, you will learn about Dean Martin like you never have before, in no time at all.

Jerry Lewis in 1981.

Jerry Lewis (1927-)

"I've had great success being a total idiot." – Jerry Lewis

Jerry Lewis has been in show business for over 7 decades, a multi-talented entertainer known for comedy, acting, singing, and producing and directing films to match. In many ways, his versatility is unprecedented even today, an era in which stars routinely alternate between film and musical careers, and Lewis has enjoyed it, as he once happily noted, "I get paid for what most kids get punished for." He has been paid in several ways, including with too many lifetime awards to count, and he remains a household name today.

At the same time, however, Lewis remains best known for his work with Dean Martin, and in that sense, he remains overshadowed by his more famous partner. There's no doubt part of this was due to the stark contrast between their images, as Martin was suave and traditionally masculine while Lewis was a bundle of frantic energy. Although the circumstances that initiated their partnership are unusual and purely coincidental, the natural contrasts between the two ensured a perfect and complementary comedic fit. Working as "Martin and Lewis", the team became the most popular nightclub act in America, commanding huge fees for their appearances all across the country.

Perhaps the most ironic aspect of their success is that Dean Martin was not a comedian in any real sense of the word, and even during their act, he essentially served as the straight man to Jerry Lewis. The routine ensured that critics took more notice of Jerry Lewis, who intentionally came across as an awkward figure with a brand of bodily humor that was borrowed from a lineage of Yiddish humor predicated on physical slapstick. And just as Martin benefited from Lewis' comedic skills, Lewis also further developed a singing career thanks to the more famous Martin's crooning.

Dean Martin and Jerry Lewis profiles the life and career of one of America's most famous entertainers. Along with pictures of important people, places, and events, you will learn about Jerry Lewis like never before, in no time at all.

Chapter 1: Dean Martin's Early Years

"Motivation is a lot of crap." – Dean Martin

"Milton Berle is an inspiration to every young person that wants to get into show business. Hard work, perseverance, and discipline: all the things you need...when you have no talent." – Dean Martin

All Americans are familiar with the name Dean Martin, but it was a name that he adopted only after entering show business. Dino Paul Crocetti was born on June 7, 1917, the son of Italian immigrants. His father Gaetano (Guy) was from Montesilvano, a small village on the coast of the Adriatic Sea, while his mother Angela was of Neapolitan and Sicilian descent. Gaetano arrived at Ellis Island in 1913, and Angela arrived one year later, but they married in 1914 when they were still just kids. Gaetano was 20 and Angela was just 16. They also wasted little time starting a family, with their first son Bill coming before Dino.

Martin and his parents

Employment prospects were relatively slim for Gaetano; who didn't have the formal education required for a good job. Like many of his Italian compatriots, he left New York and headed west, stopping at Steubenville, Ohio. At the time, Steubenville was a focal point of the steel industry; thanks to its location just 35 miles away from Pittsburgh, the steel capital of the United States. Steubenville was an industrial hotbed for manufacturing, which may not have made for a glamorous line of work but needed all the help it could get. As a farmhand from Italy, Gaetano was accustomed enough to manual labor, and his two older brothers had already arrived in Ohio. It was a foregone conclusion that Gaetano would join them.

Angela's background differed substantially from that of her future husband. She was raised by German nuns, and though she held a strong sense of national pride, her upbringing had been more tranquil than her husband's. She was quiet, especially compared to her son, and she opened her own business as a seamstress, working from home. Instead of moving to Steubenville upon arriving in the United States, she settled in Fernwood, Ohio, a town located roughly 200 miles away.

Although Gaetano worked in the steel mills immediately after arriving in Steubenville, he eventually became a barber, a profession for which he was passionate. He and Angela raised their family in Steubenville, and although the small city held a rough flavor, the family lived in a friendly working-class neighborhood. Describing Steubenville, Martin's son Ricci explained the mix between congeniality and hard labor that typified the citizens: "Its residents mixed heartland patriotism with scraped knuckles and a dirt-under-the-fingernails work ethic. And at the end of the day, they knew how to have a good time." The town was far from affluent, but Gaetano's barber shop was a fixture, and the steady stream of scraggly steel mill workers provided constant business.

Gaetano and Angela raised their family with a strong sense of national pride. In fact, Italian was the spoken language in their household, and Dean did not learn English until after starting school. He entered Grant Elementary school in Steubenville, and he went on to attend Steubenville High School. From the beginning, Dean was never a strong or committed student, possibly due in large part to the fact that he could barely speak English when he began his education. His lack of familiarity made him an easy target for ridicule, as he was routinely chided for his bad English throughout elementary school. Finally, in the 10th grade, Martin quit school altogether, ending his education at Steubenville High. Always a wisecrack, Martin quipped that he was smarter than his teachers anyway.

Most descriptions of Martin's education cast his childhood in an excessively negative light. While he was certainly no scholar, Dean's upbringing was generally healthy and supportive. Not only was his biological extended family close-knit, but his neighborhood was close-knit and essentially doubled as a second family. As a child, Martin pursued a variety of hobbies, including playing bocce ball, singing in a choir, and being a boy scout. For better or worse, Martin's proclivity for leisure, something that would become a hallmark of sorts, played a strong role in precluding active engagement in his formal education. Instead of studying, he would go to watch movies, spend time in pool-rooms, and frequent nightclubs. The late 1920s and 1930s were a period of rapid growth in the motion picture industry, and Martin was as captivated as the rest of the nation. Films had just entered the era of synchronized sound, and in a sense Martin was able to better perfect his still-deficient English by watching films instead of in a more formal classroom environment, where his shoddy English was fodder for ridicule.

Martin's parents were able to tolerate their son dropping out of high school by placing a premium on hard work and impressing upon him the necessity to enter the workforce. Gaetano had always hoped his son would join him at the barber shop, but Dean was not exactly thrilled by that prospect. For a short time, he worked in the steel industry, which seems comical in retrospect, and it is unsurprising that he could not handle the brutal labor. He quit that job quickly, and he spent the remainder of his teenage years pursuing a variety of jobs that were loosely affiliated with the entertainment industry. He even took up boxing as a 15 year old, despite being just 135 pounds, fighting under the nickname "Kid Crochet", a play off his last name. He stuck at it long enough to batter his hands and suffer a broken nose, but he was so wildly unsuccessful that he later joked that he fought 12 times and "won all but 11" of them. One humorous legend claims that he would take money to box with his roommate and future Italian-American hit singer Sonny King in their apartment until one of them was knocked out.

Sonny King

Eventually, Martin worked as a roulette stickman and croupier in an illegal casino, which seems like a natural fit for him since the members of the Rat Pack were notorious for frequenting gambling establishments. Nonetheless, it's remarkable that Dean was able to secure such employment even at such a young age. He later said of his work, "I can't stand an actor or actress who tells me acting is hard work. It's easy work. Anyone who says it isn't never had to stand on his feet all day dealing blackjack."

For the most part, the first two decades of Martin's life were not productive. His fun-loving personality was endearing to those around him, but he did not commit himself to either his studies or his jobs. Thankfully, that all changed beginning in 1934, when he began performing music for the first time.

During the summer of that year, Martin performed at Craig Beach, Ohio, and from the start he showed a great deal of talent and charisma. By this point in his career, Martin had not yet developed his style, but like Sinatra, he borrowed from the crooning musical styles of singers like Harry Mills and Bing Crosby. Even though his singing career was still in its beginning stages, Martin had an innate ability to charm an audience; he was extraordinarily good looking, and his pronounced Italian accent was a natural fit for the Ohioan demographic.

Bing Crosby

Martin continued to sing during summers while he worked as a boxer and roulette stickman, but he increasingly viewed those as temporary odd jobs on the way to being a singer. In the spring of 1939, his career began to take off after he performed at the Mounds Club in Lake County, Ohio. Performing for a wider audience earned him greater attention, and he was subsequently hired to join the Ernie McKay band in Columbus, his first major break.

When he was hired by the Ernie McKay band, he was instructed to change his name to "Dino Martino," a title that played off the fame of the Metropolitan Opera singer Nino Martini. There is no denying that "Dino Martini" has a catchier ring to it than Dino Crocetti, but the new designation still retained his Italian ethnicity. The new name conferred a certain exoticism to his image, but it still did so within the relatively narrow constraints of an explicitly Italian identity. It was also in keeping with his laid-back and fun-loving reputation, as the last name certainly reminded listeners of the drink too.

Performing with the Ernie McKay band was a major career development for Martin, but the following year his career reached even greater significance. In 1940, he was discovered by Sammy Watkins and eventually hired to join the Sammy Watkins Orchestra. However, Watkins did not care for the name "Dino Martini", and when he hired Crocetti in the fall of 1940, he insisted that the singer change his name to the very Americana "Dean Martin". The 23 year old had just been given his famous name.

Immediately after joining the Sammy Watkins orchestra, Martin performed with the group in the Cleveland area. Over time, he would perform on the road with the band, and they played all over the country. Signing with Watkins brought Martin his highest-ever salary, earning what was then a healthy $50 per week.

Martin's burgeoning career also corresponded with developments in his personal life. While singing in Cleveland, he met Betty MacDonald, a young lady from Swarthmore, Pennsylvania who was staying with her father in Cleveland. McDonald was just out of high school when she first met Dean. A strong, athletic woman who had been a lacrosse star, Betty's Irish heritage was obviously different than Martin's Italian background, but Martin was not deterred by her background. At the time, the Irish were held in equal if not higher regard than Italians, and Martin did not share the fierce Italian patriotism held by many immigrants and first-generation Italian-Americans. Never a shy gentleman, Martin courted her immediately, proposed to her just a few weeks after meeting her, and married here in Cleveland in October 1941. The couple took up residency in Cleveland Heights.

The itinerant lifestyle of the musical performer made domestic life especially difficult for the young couple. When Dean went off on extended road trips, Betty was left with little to keep her occupied. But in 1942, she and Martin had their first child when Stephan (later known as Craig) was born that summer. Martin's career also experienced a significant milestone in 1942, when he performed with the Sammy Watkins Orchestra for NBC on their broadcast of the "Fitch Bandwagon." It was the first time a national audience got a view of Martin, but he was still not making a great deal of money, a situation exacerbated by the fact his family was growing.

Martin in 1943

It has long been speculated that Martin's early singing career was helped in large part by connections to the Mafia, including with Chicago boss Sam Giancana. Entire books have been written on the alleged relationship between Martin and the mob. Characterizations of Martin's ties to the Chicago mob have ranged from being considered nonexistent to a big reason he got his break in show business. As with Sinatra, it's likely the truth was somewhere in-between; it was possible for Italian-Americans to have a friendly relationship with goodfellas and not be part of the mob.

Martin's career received another big boost when he was hired by the MCA talent agency in 1943. With that, he was able to perform at greater venues than before, finally acquiring the type of broad audience that facilitated national acclaim. Moreover, Martin became his own entity, freeing himself from the inherent restrictions of performing in a group. At long last, he was free to perfect his style in whichever way he saw fit. Around the same time, Frank Sinatra had become the most famous singer in America, and he had also broken out on his own in 1943, making what was then a virtually unprecedented move by performing as a soloist. In this vein, Martin's early career effectively mirrored Sinatra. Although he was not releasing any records (while Sinatra was), Martin's elevating stardom certainly owed a great deal to his future Rat Pack partner-in-crime.

From the beginning, Martin offered a fresh alternative to Sinatra. Although Sinatra had begun his career as a crooner, he transitioned to more showy tunes at a time in which Martin was perfecting the crooning style that would make him famous. Martin was also more visibly Italian than Sinatra, due to his swarthier skin complexion and far more pronounced accent. The two were similar, however, in that neither was formally trained as a singer and could not read sheet music.

Martin and Sinatra

Martin's early years as a solo performer were not entirely successful, however, In 1943, he was called upon to perform at the prestigious Riobamba club in New York City, and since he was still considered a relatively minor talent, he was a last-minute replacement for Sinatra. Unfortunately, Martin became overwhelmed by the situation, and his performance was an enormous failure. In retrospect, this performance is surprising since it is difficult to even envision Martin in a nervous state. In fact, his image as a relaxed, half-drunk but nevertheless charming performer was the result of years of familiarity performing before large audiences. To his credit, Martin continued to find steady employment even after the debacle.

By 1944, Martin had risen to the forefront of the entertainment industry. In January of that year, he appeared on the cover of *Billboard* magazine, and his calm façade was a refreshing antidote to the anxieties that filled wartime America. However, like many performers, Martin was drafted and called upon to serve in World War II in 1944. He was stationed in Akron, Ohio, but unbeknownst to him, Martin was suffering from a hernia at this time, and after just one year in the service he was classified as 4-F and discharged. Martin had never been enthusiastic about entering the service in the first place, and the discharge was a fortuitous development in his career. While other stars were off fighting overseas or training in the United States, Martin was able to work on his career and increase his popularity.

In March of 1944, Dean and Betty had a second child, a daughter named Claudia. Having a second child would suggest that Dean was becoming increasingly committed to being a family man, but in fact the exact opposite was true. As he became more famous, Martin had numerous affairs, and his traveling lifestyle offered the perfect opportunity for one-night stands. With legions of adoring fans, Martin had a captive audience, and his wife was not there to keep tabs on her husband. Martin's status as a poor family man surfaced in other ways too; he was irresponsible with the money he made and failed to adequately provide for Betty and the two children. The vast majority of the money he earned was spent immediately after it was received, forcing Betty to live frugally while her husband gallivanted around the country.

Martin's wife and kids weren't the only people who suffered from his financial mismanagement. In fact, after he signed with MCA, he decided to have a nose job to fix the damage done years earlier by boxing. However, he had been unable to save up the money to have the operation. He resorted to borrowing money for the operation, but then he spent the money he had borrowed. He got the nose job in August of 1944, but only after he had reached deals with so many talent agents that he had somehow managed to sign away over a substantial amount of his income.

Fortunately for Martin, his talent was able to compensate for his persistent inability to manage his funds. In August of 1944, shortly after getting his nose fixed, Martin was able to acquire his own radio show, a major accomplishment in an era in which the radio was just beginning to supplant cinema as the privileged form of entertainment in the United States. From the mid-1940s through the 1950s, more private forms of entertainment gained in popularity against the movie theater and baseball stadium. Even if it did not allow him to take advantage of his good looks, Martin's easy, crooning voice was a natural fit for the radio, and his fame only continued to grow.

Chapter 2: A Born Performer

"I need the applause." – Jerry Lewis

Joseph Levitch was born on March 16, 1926 in Newark, New Jersey to parents who had come from Russia as children because of that country's persecution of Jewish peasants. They were both in show business, with his father, Daniel, acting as a Master of Ceremonies for a local vaudeville house and his mother, Rachel, playing the piano for radio station WOR in New York City and accompanying her husband's show. Since immigrants were often looked down upon in early 20th century America, the Levitch's worked under the stages names of Danny and Rae Lewis. As an adult, Jerry Lewis explained how his parents' professions affected his childhood and his own ambitions:

> "I was a lonely kid, the only child of two vaudevillians who were rarely around. My dad, Danny, was a singer and all-around entertainer: he did it all—patter, impressions, stand-up comedy. My mom, Rachel (Rae), was Danny's pianist and conductor. So I grew up shuttled from household to household, relative to relative. I cherished the precious times Mom and Dad would take me on the road with them. And for them, the highest form of togetherness was to put me right in the act; my first onstage appearance was at age five, in 1931, at the President's Hotel, a summer resort in Swan Lake, New York. I wore a tux (naturally) and sang that Depression classic 'Brother, Can You Spare a Dime?' From that moment on, showbiz was in my blood. So was loneliness."

Like his parents, Joseph's name was also Americanized to Joey Lewis when he made his stage debut in 1931. By this time, the Great Depression was in full swing, so his childlike rendition of "Brother, Can You Spare a Dime" was a big hit with audiences. Before long, he was making the rounds on New York's famous Borscht Circuit, a theater district catering to Russian immigrants, and even when he was just 15, he was making enough money performing at nightclubs and burlesque shows to justify, at least in his own mind, pursuing a career in entertainment. As a result, he left Irvington High School and changed his name to Jerry Lewis to avoid confusion with Joe E. Lewis, who was already a well-known and established comedian.

Joe E. Lewis

Of course, breaking into the business is always a lot easier said than done, and Lewis recounted some of the dues he had to pay coming up: "I worked the Catskill resorts as a busboy (for pay) and (for free) a tummler—the guy who cuts up, makes faces, gets the guests in a good mood for the real entertainment. That's what I wanted to be, the real entertainment. But what was I going to do? I was tall, skinny, gawky; cute but funny-looking With the voice God had given me, I certainly wasn't going to be a singer like my dad, with his Al Jolson baritone. I always saw the humor in things, the joke possibilities. At the same time, I didn't have the confidence to stand on a stage and talk."

Nevertheless, once his decision was made, Lewis set about proving it was the right one. Dressed in a drape jacket reminiscent of his Russian forebears and the pegged pants popular with entertainers at that time, Lewis visited one booking office after another, until he finally got a job performing as part of a burlesque show in Buffalo, New Jersey. Inspired, Lewis continued to develop an act built around lip-syncing to songs played on a backstage record player. Using a routine that was more comedic that professional, he made his now famous faces, as well as exaggerated body movements, to songs ranging from popular to operatic, but after a few weeks there, he began to think he had made a mistake. He was young and away from home for the first time, so he eventually considered packing it in and returning to Newark.

Discouraged, he shared his thoughts with Max Coleman, a longtime member of the burlesque comedy circuit, but Coleman, who was also an old friend of Lewis' father, saw something in the young man and told him so. Coleman encouraged him to stay where he was and continue working in the field, so the following summer, Lewis opened a new act, this time performing as a mime in Lock Sheldrake, New York. His show at Brown's Hotel was a hit and caught the eyes of Irving Kaye, himself a veteran of the Borscht Circuit. Kaye subsequently took Lewis under his wing and used his own connections to get the young man more bookings, and the two men would remain lifelong friends.

When Lewis turned 18 in March 1944, World War II was reaching its climax, but when he tried to enlist, the doctors discovered a heart murmur that made him unfit for duty. That allowed him to keep performing, and he also married Patti Palmer in October. Born Esther Calonico, Palmer was a singer with Ted Fio Rito when she and Lewis met, and having little ambition beyond being a wife and mother, she abandoned her career after they were married and was soon pregnant with their first child, Gary, who was born in July 1945. He and his wife hoped that other children would follow him, but after several years, they began to believe there would be no more babies, so they adopted Ronald Steven in 1950. Lewis later recounted what it was like living in America just after the war: "Please realize that these were very uncertain times. No matter how many images you conjure of the triumphant armies marching home, the sailor kissing the girl in Times Square, the years just after the war were dark and uncertain ones. Millions had been killed and maimed…Meanwhile, our G.I.s, back from the war, were encouraged to embrace peace and prosperity. Everybody was supposed to get into harness and turn the U.S.A. into paradise on earth. There was a lot of unease and rebellion just under the country's placid surface."

However, by this time, Lewis had also met the man who would change his life, though he didn't know it yet. He later described the scene: "[He] smiled warmly and put out his hand. I took it. It was a big hand, strong, but he didn't go overboard with the grip. I liked that. I liked him, instantly. And he looked genuinely glad to meet me…[My friend] had zero idea that he was introducing me to one of the great comic talents of our time. I certainly had no idea of that, either—nor, for that matter, did Dean. At that moment, at the end of World War II, we were just two guys struggling to make it in show business, shaking hands on a busy Broadway street corner." In his memoir *Dean and Me: A Love Story*, Lewis also explained how his first encounter with Martin left him awestruck: "Just looking at him intimidated me: How does anybody get that handsome? I smiled at the sight of him in that camel's hair coat. Harry Horseshit, I thought. That was what we used to call a guy who thought he was smooth with the ladies…But this guy I knew, was the real deal."

It would be another year before the two actually appeared together anywhere, and even that was unplanned. While they were both at the Havana-Madrid nightclub in March 1946, Lewis decided late one night to pull a prank on Martin. He interrupted Martin's singing act with a silly prank that delighted the audience. These random interruptions became a regular occurrence, and Martin began to fight back, pulling pranks on Lewis and heckling him back. According to Lewis, "We were just screwing around, really, but an eerily farsighted journalist named Bill Smith sensed that something was cooking. 'Martin and Lewis do an after-piece that has all the makings of a sock act,' he wrote in Billboard. 'Boys plays straight for each other, deliberately step on each other's lines, mug and raise general bedlam. It's a toss-up who walks off with the biggest mitt. Lewis's double-takes, throw-aways, mugging and deliberate over-acting are sensational. Martin's slow takes, ad libs and under-acting make him an ideal fall guy. Both got stand-out results from a mob that took dynamite to wake up.'"

The "screwing around" would indeed be the beginning of something amazing, but not right away. Instead, it would all come together a few months later when Lewis was at Atlantic City's 500 Club. One of the performers in the show quit, so Lewis recommended that Martin be hired to replace him. The two went on stage separately on July 24, 1946, but there was no magic, no doubt in part due to the fact Martin had no comedic acting experience. However, between the first and second performances, Lewis outlined a new act on the back of the paper wrapper his pastrami sandwich had come in. Instead of performing more "sophisticated" humor, they performed a purely improvised slapstick routine that won over the audience. Martin sang and dropped all pretense of being a serious comedian, while Lewis acted like a goof. The two went on again with the show that Lewis had created, and it was a hit. With that, their comedy partnership was born.

Chapter 3: Martin and Lewis

Dean Martin and Jerry Lewis

"Postwar America was a very buttoned-up nation. Radio shows were run by censors, Presidents wore hats, ladies wore girdles. We came straight out of the blue - nobody was expecting anything like Martin and Lewis. A sexy guy and a monkey is how some people saw us." – Jerry Lewis

After they perfected their act at the 500, the two received offers to play nightclubs up and down the East Coast. Following their initial appearance together, Martin and Lewis reprised their routine at the 500 Club in Atlantic City, and it was there that they became acknowledged as a comedy team. Their rise to fame was swift, and they began headlining programs and commanding salaries of $1200 per week. Their first performance as "Martin and Lewis" occurred at the Loew's State Theater in New York City in 1947, where their weekly salary was $1500. By the following year, they commanded the extraordinary sum of $12,000 per week and were featured at elite venues like the Copacabana in New York City. Their performances set attendance records, and highbrow and lowbrow celebrities alike jockeyed for valuable seats in order to watch the duo in person, including film icon Humphrey Bogart. To those who criticized his singing performances in the comedy routines, Martin shot back, "You wanna hear it straight, buy the album."

An early Martin and Lewis Performance

By the time Martin and Lewis did a gig at New York City's famous Copacabana Club in April 1948, they were being paid $2,500 a show, a princely sum in those days. Of course, that amount was well worth it, because their audiences were keeling over with laughter. The two would later claim that their success lay in ignoring their audience and just playing off each other. The chemistry worked, and the team was approached by the famous producer Hal Wallis about a Hollywood movie contract. While their agent put Wallis off, it was only a matter of time until they made their first movie. At the same time, Martin's singing career continued, which helped ensure that Lewis would be included; in 1948, they signed with Capitol Records, where they recorded the hit song "That Certain Party."

Wallis

Meanwhile, their comedy act was still going strong, and their next big gig was at Slapie Maxie's in Los Angeles in August 1948. As soon as the Hollywood bigwigs heard about their performance, the contract offers piled up, but Wallis finally won out and signed them to a 5 year contract with Paramount Studios. By then, they had appeared on television together in June 1948 on Ed Sullivan's *Toast of the Town* on CBS, and they subsequently appeared on NBC's *Welcome Aboard* in October.

At this point, Martin and Lewis were enormously popular within the entertainment industry, and they had the benefit of not being tied to the kind of contractual obligations that plagued most actors during the time period. When the duo signed their contract, the studio system was still very much in place in Hollywood, and most actors effectively served as indentured servants, forced to appear in whichever films their parent studio decided and typecast as the studio saw fit. For the most part, Martin and Lewis were slated to appear in films directed by Hal Willis, but they were also given the freedom to appear in one outside film each year. Even better, they were allowed control over all of their other entertainment appearances. The leverage they had garnered from their fame performing live thus ensured a very comfortable arrangement within the motion picture industry, and they enjoyed privileges that were unheard of for all other actors just entering the film industry.

Martin and Lewis spent the spring of 1949 filming their first picture together, *My Friend Irma.* Originally, it intended to cast Martin as Steve, a singer who falls in love with a money-loving woman but must also contend with Lewis' character. However, while Lewis was supposed to play a character called Al, he was ultimately judged unsuited for the part. Determined not to be separated from Martin, Lewis invented a sidekick for Martin's character, and as a result, Seymour was written into the script. This proved to be a wise move, since at least one critic, writing for *The New York Times*, did not care for the movie but praised Lewis' performance:

> "We could go along with the laughs which were fetched by a new mad comedian, Jerry Lewis by name. This freakishly built and acting young man, who has been seen in night clubs hereabouts with a collar-ad partner, Dean Martin, has a genuine comic quality. The swift eccentricity of his movements, the harrowing features of his face and the squeak of his vocal protestations, which are many and frequent, have flair. His idiocy constitutes a burlesque of an idiot, which, is something else again. As a hanger-on in the wake of Irma, he's the funniest thing in this film.
>
> Indeed, he's the only thing in it that we can expressly propose as a reason for seeing the picture. Hal Wallis, the producer, cast him well. For as much as one may like his partner, Mr. Martin, and his Bing-Crosby style, one has to remark that he gives forth only standard glamour in this film. And his singing, a la Mr. Crosby, is able but well this side of Bing's. (...) By using his wits to play an ignoramus, he somewhat brightens a very dopey film."

After *My Friend Irma* made a splash at the box office, Paramount decided to quickly release a sequel, *My Friend Irma Goes West*. It turned out to be a wise decision, because while the original opened to mixed reviews, the sequel was an unmitigated success. As one reviewer pointed out:

> "The only people who had trouble smiling yesterday in the Paramount Theatre were the ushers and the cashiers. They were too preoccupied handling the overflow crowds to notice what was going on up on the screen. In fact, we had a bit of trouble, too, keeping track of the dialogue which fills in the gaps between sight gags in "My Friend Irma Goes West" because the audience was having a laughing spell. During the first ten minutes of this helter-skelter comedy we missed most of Jerry Lewis' witty remarks, for every time he opened his mouth the audience went into hysterics. There were a lot of young, high squeaking voices bouncing off the rafters, but while the small fry may have been most responsive they did not account for all the merry sounds.
>
> Jerry Lewis, the slight, abject, elastic young man, and his straight-man-accomplice with the velvety baritone singing voice, Dean Martin, are responsible for about ninety-nine and nine-tenths of the fun in 'My Friend Irma Goes West.'"

When *At War with the Army* came out in late 1950, it was not the hit that everyone had hoped for. Martin and Lewis had agreed to make the film for very small salaries in exchange for a 90% share of the film's net profits, but after a lengthy legal struggle trying to get their fair share of the money, the two gave up and surrendered their rights to the profits. Though it was based on a play by the same name, the producers of the movie added several sequences, including one of Lewis dressed as a woman and another hilarious take on the actors trying to make their way through an obstacle course. They also added several songs that Martin could perform, some with Lewis. One reviewer observed an obvious truth:

> "The boys, for the record, are doing what they have been doing naturally on the radio and in the bistros. They are pals in civilian life who have switched their operations to a training camp, with Dean Martin a singing-and-skirt-chasing first sergeant and the woebegone Jerry Lewis a bungling private. (…) Mr. Lewis does nobly in several pantomimic turns, using his mobile features and lean frame with telling effect. And, both partners contribute their well-known and, for this corner's money, best bit in impersonating Bing Crosby and Barry Fitzgerald as the priests of 'Going My Way.' Mr. Lewis also gets things going with a bang in a number titled, 'The Navy Gets the Gravy But the Army Gets the Beans.' It's a prophetic start. For, without Mr. Lewis, beans is what this viewer got."

When Martin and Lewis were offered the chance to host a weekly television show in 1950, they jumped at the opportunity. Soon, they were starring every Sunday night in *The Colgate Comedy Hour*. This was one of many variety shows that were popular on television during the 1950s, and they remained with the show until it was cancelled in 1955. During those five years, they had a chance to meet and work with some of the biggest names in comedy.

Martin and Lewis on *The Colgate Comedy Hour*

All the while, the pair kept making movies, and Lewis received rave reviews for his role as a hapless football player in *That's My Boy*, even if the movie itself did not: "Heredity, heroes, football and pure corn have been mixed vigorously in 'That's My Boy' but this film concoction, which arrived at the Paramount yesterday is not heady. There are occasional moments when the mixture, spiked by the mugging of Jerry Lewis, does have its special lift. By and large, however, this latest excursion into amiable insanity by the team of Dean Martin and Jerry Lewis is a labored repetition of one situation."

The same sort of enthusiasm greeted his role in *Sailor Beware*, another Hal Willis film that featured Martin and Lewis as Al and Melvin, sailors who meet in the Navy recruiting line. Al has previously been rejected from the service due to his bad knees, while Melvin enters the service because he is allergic to women's fragrances and is ordered by a doctor to acquire sea travel. They are each admitted into the Navy, and the plot features the basic template for the Martin and Lewis films of the decade. Dean and Jerry act like a couple, with Martin playing the role of the virile man and Lewis the almost infantile son (or spouse). *Sailor Beware* also placed great emphasis on the striking physical, intellectual, and cultural differences between the pair. Constantly stuttering and stumbling about, Lewis appears very much as the homely comic, while Martin fulfills his image as a suave man, but as the narrative progresses, Martin facilitates Lewis's maturation into the role of the confident heterosexual male. Much of the comedy in the films was based on the unlikelihood of Lewis ever attracting the women with whom he comes into contact in the films, but viewers were persuaded to gaze in wonder at his remarkable growth into the role of ladies' man. One reviewer explained:

> "Mr. Lewis—who is, of course, the funnier one—pops into the old comic routine of the frightened tyro tossed into the boxing ring with the tough and forbidding fighter, the comedy has style, for Mr. Lewis is a grotesque pantomimist and he strikes some hilarious attitudes. His fast and elaborate footwork to stay away from his baffled foe, while he shadowboxes like sixty, is graphic and genuine fun. (…) Mr. Lewis is also on the right track in the earlier part of the film when he gives a stripped-down impersonation of a Navy recruit being given his medical exam. His expressions of stupid amazement when the doctors find his so-called blood is clear and that his heart-beat does not even register are neatly and cleverly timed to his subsequent outburst of horror when a workman comes at him with a drill. Mr. Lewis, an oddly built specimen, is aware that he has a funny face."

Sometimes it is the small things that mark true success. Lewis won the Photoplay Award and was nominated for a Primetime Emmy for Best Comedian or Comedienne in 1952, but to him, nothing represented success like he and Martin being asked to make a cameo appearance in Bob Hope and Bing Crosby's *Road to Bali.* Comfortable with the film process, Lewis also expanded his career by co-writing a movie, *The Stooge*, and though he received no public credit for his work, he had a hit. He and Martin filmed the movie in the winter of 1951, but Paramount was reluctant to release it because the way in which the film portrayed Martin's treatment of Lewis. Ironically, when it was finally released, it became Lewis' favorite of his movies, but their first dramatic film was not very well received, with one reviewer observing, "Now, we don't want to take the position that Mr. Martin and Mr. Lewis could not play a straight dramatic show, if they wanted.… But the mixture of slapstick and sentiment that is tossed off in 'The Stooge' is a little bewildering for them, not to mention their customers. The going gets rather sticky and unfunny toward the end. This is not only oddly depressing; it is perilous to one's simple faith in man."

Martin and Lewis also spent December 1951 and January 1952 filming *Jumping Jacks*, a movie based on a story originally written by Robert Lees and Fred Rinaldo during World War II, but before Paramount could complete it, the war ended and army comedies fell out of favor. A reviewer noted, “The Ripping and Roaring Society of Jerry Lewis Fans…was rolling in the aisles and generally acting in its customarily warm, responsive way at the opening performance of their hero's new picture, ‘Jumping Jacks,’ in that theatre yesterday. (…) …the whooping and hollering of the audience at the Paramount yesterday was such as to make these demonstrations seem the crowning achievement of comic art. These and other exercises of Mr. Lewis in the film...were greeted with such enthusiasm that one can only inquire, what has happened to the standards of humor, even those of Jerry Lewis fans?”

Scared Stiff, released in 1953, was a remake of a Bob Hope classic, *The Ghost Breakers* (1940), and just as they had appeared in cameos in *Road to Bali*, Hope and Crosby made cameo appearances in *Scared Stiff*. Martin and Lewis did not want to make the movie since they thought the original was good enough to be left alone, but Wallis believed they could breathe new life into it and insisted that they appear in it. The two worked on it during the first half of the summer of 1952, dealing with the delays caused by new technology; *Scared Stiff* was the first movie they made that was filmed with the new, cutting edge 3-stack stereo sound. Some critics felt that the improved sound quality made the film’s comedic scenes funnier, but modern viewers have no way of knowing because the tracks were lost.

Even though these movies were getting mixed reviews, Martin and Lewis were household names and as famous as ever, The fact that the two men had achieved such fame together is remarkable given that Dean Martin was not a comedian, and it’s fair to wonder whether Martin and Lewis would have ever risen to fame without the other. As Lewis himself put it, “Who were Dean's fans? Men, women, the Italians. Who were Jerry's fans? Women, Jews, kids. Who were Martin and Lewis' fans? All of them... You had fans that didn't give a shit that Jerry was on or that Dean was singing. Because if Dean was singing, that was Martin and Lewis. If Jerry was goin' nuts, that was Martin and Lewis." Regardless, the duo was in fact so popular that when DC Comics issued a series of comic books called *The Adventures of Dean Martin and Jerry Lewis*, they were bestsellers from 1952 until the team split up in 1957. DC Comics later published the equally popular *The Adventures of Jerry Lewis* through 1971, which led to a cartoon series in 1970 called *Will the Real Jerry Lewis Please Sit Down.*

Chapter 4: Lewis and Martin

Martin and Lewis on *The Colgate Comedy Hour* in 1955.

"It was complicated. …everything between two human beings is complicated! And in a relationship like Dean and I had (which was unlike any relationship I've ever known), it was much, much more so." – Jerry Lewis

Always looking for a new angle with which to promote a movie, Paramount had Martin and Lewis record a radio promotion for their next film, *The Caddy*. Ironically, the two were not used to making such recordings and had a problem getting their collective lines straight. In fact, some recordings of their attempts, complete with the long strings of profanity that following each failure, were included on *The Golden Age of Comedy: Dean Martin and Jerry Lewis* CD.

Nonetheless, *Caddy Shack* would arguably become the duo's most famous movie together. The film was just the second (after *At War with the Army* (1950)) that was produced by York Pictures Corporation, a production company that the pair had purchased at the start of the decade. Directed by Norman Taurog, the film features Martin as Joe, a golfer who benefits from the advice of Harvey (Lewis), the son of a famous golf professional. Harvey caddies for Joe, but later in the film, they decide to go into show business together and eventually meet the real-life Martin and Lewis. The plot contains some biographical elements, including the sheer coincidence that brought Martin and Lewis together as performers, and the film is also highlighted by a show stopping production of "That's Amore," which became an immediate sensation. Moreover, the film is significant for exposing their actual personas; it was exceedingly rare for a film to make reference to the actual personas of the actors performing the characters. The fact that the film "breaks the fourth wall" reflects the confidence the studio held in the Martin and Lewis brand, as well as the status wielded by the duo.

Martin and Lewis in *The Caddy*

Following the release of *The Caddy* in 1953, the pair began work on *Money From Home*, their only foray into 3-D movies and their first color film. Unfortunately, the technology used in 3-D filming was still new, so there were problems with the initial limited release on December 31, 1953, but the bugs were worked out by the time the movie went into general release in February 1954. Though Lewis co-wrote and co-directed a number of pictures, *Money From Home* was the only movie in which he received any sort of on-screen credit: "Special Material in Song Numbers Staged by Jerry Lewis."

Critics continued to praise Lewis's performances, saying of his role in *Living It Up*, "…Mr. Lewis' needle-sharp impersonation of three foreign medicos, in a hospital sequence, is a piece of comic artistry. With his sights imaginatively set, this little guy has no peer." However, while everyone was raving about Lewis' performances, more and more critics were either ignoring Martin or being critical of his work, and things between the two men came to a head in 1954, when they did a cover shoot for *Look* magazine. They were both interviewed and photographed together, along with their co-star in *Living It Up*, Sheree North, but when the magazine was finally released, Martin's face had been cropped from the cover, infuriating the actor. While Lewis agreed with him about being offended, there was little that he, as the rising star, could do to fix things. It was the beginning of the end of their partnership.

In 1955, Martin and Lewis appeared in two films that did quite well at the box office, but one is considerably more acclaimed today than the other. First, they acted together in *You're Never Too Young* (1955), in which Jerry appears as Wilbur Lewis, a young man who pretends to be 11 years old in order to receive the children's price for the train fare. While on the train, he meets and falls in love with a schoolteacher who mistakes him for a child and gives him attention. Martin appears in the film as Bob Miles, fiancée to Nancy.

The film is relatively minor within Martin's personal filmography, but it amply demonstrated the shifting dynamics in the partnership. In this film, it's clear that Lewis is the main character, and Martin's role as straight man is largely ceded to the schoolteacher. Furthermore, unlike most of their other films, they both compete for the love of the same woman, meaning their partnership on film no longer exists to nurture Lewis' transformation into a man capable of courting a female. Lewis retains his trademark infantilism, but unlike the earlier films, the viewer gets the distinct impression that Martin's appearance in the film is largely tangential.

The more revered film in 1955 was *Artists and Models*, which stands alongside *The Caddy* in discussions of the most renowned of the Martin and Lewis films. Dean appears as Rick, a painter and ladies man, while Jerry appears as Eugene, Rick's roommate, and as in their earlier films, the two characters are polar opposites. Rick is suave and calm, but Eugene conveys a constant, frantic energy. Rick's job as a painter aligns him with traditional "higher" forms of art, but Eugene is obsessed with comic books, which were regarded as more of a juvenile obsession than they are today. That the two characters are devoted to forms of graphic art is significant, as the film's highly-saturated colors and overall lavish visual style assume a comic book (or paint canvas) quality. Lewis was particularly gratified to get to work with Frank Tashlin, one of his idols and directors of the famous *Looney Tunes* cartoons, and viewers could recognize some of the *Looney Tunes* gags in the movies, including a steaming water cooler and a very overextended massage. Tashlin also introduced a level of sexual innuendo and skimpy costumes to the picture that had been absent from the pair's previous films; in fact, there were a number of jokes that Paramount was unable to get past the censors.

Tashlin

The plot of *Artists and Models* harkens back to the earlier films between the pair, as Martin assumes the role of partner and caretaker for the hyper Lewis. In fact, Lewis' sense of space and scale throughout the film is even more disorderly than in the earlier films. He relies on Martin in the manner that a pet relies on his owner, and an improbable romance develops between Eugene and the female comic book author who lives in their building due in large part to Rick's influence. At the same time, however, *Artists and Models* is similar to *You're Never Too Young* in that it subordinates Martin to focus on Lewis. In earlier films, Martin was permitted to assume equal or even greater prominence than his co-star, like with his arresting performance of "That's Amore" in *The Caddy*, but as the 1950s progressed, friction continued to grow as Martin became acutely aware that he was essentially a straight-guy sidekick to the star attraction of Jerry Lewis. Exacerbating this dynamic was the close relationship forming between Lewis and Frank Tashlin, a pairing that in many ways replaced the partnership between Martin and Lewis. In fact, Lewis and Tashlin would appear in a number of films throughout the 1950s and the first half of the 1960s, while Martin and Lewis acted alongside each another in just two more films.

Martin and Lewis in *Artists and Models*

When it was released that November, *Artists and Models* quickly became one of the highest grossing movies of the year, and part of its popularity stemmed from its satiric treatment of many issues near and dear to the 1950s American heart. The movie poked fun at everything from the space race to violent comic books. While this was the only movie in which Shirley MacLaine appeared with both Lewis and Martin, she would go on to make a number of other pictures with the latter during the years that followed.

By 1956, the relationship between Martin and Lewis was breaking down. It was understandable that Martin was irritated about playing second fiddle to Lewis, but he also accused Lewis of changing. Martin said of Lewis, "At some point, he said to himself, 'I'm extraordinary, like Charles Chaplin.' From then on, nobody could tell him anything. He knew it all." In one legendary exchange, Martin told Lewis that Lewis was "nothing but a f****** dollar sign" to him. Lewis later explained what Martin might have been getting at, "When I would be myself, I was being big-headed. I was being egotistical. I was a megalomaniac, when it really was just having not to be a monkey for a few hours a day. And fulfilling the need to be a man."

Given the state of their relationship, it should come as no surprise that the final two movies starring Martin and Lewis were both released in 1956. In *Pardners*, the duo star as ranchers who join forces to avenge the deaths of their fathers at the hands of a group of killers. In the context of their careers, *Pardners* was far more significant for Lewis than for Martin. Martin and Lewis both play two roles, appearing as parents and the (grown) children bent on bringing their fathers' killers to justice. Although the dual roles (as fathers and then sons) are highly similar, the film was the first in a long line of movies in which Lewis performs separate roles (the most famous among these is *The Nutty Professor*, in which Lewis' alter ego character borrows heavily from Martin himself.)

Suspecting their partnership was nearing its end, Lewis brought a hand held 16 mm movie camera to the set of *Pardners*, and as 1955 turned to 1956, he filmed the duo's work together on the picture. By this time rumors were swirling that this would be their last movie together, so to discourage such speculation, the two filmed a scene in which they interrupted the closing "The End" sign. According to Lewis:

> "I yelled, 'We're not ready for "The End" yet!' Then Dean and I drew our pistols and fired, shattering each letter as if it were glass. When we were done, we stepped out of character and spoke directly to the audience.
>
> 'We have something to say to you, right, Dean?' I said.
>
> 'We sure do, Jer. We want you folks to know we sure enjoyed workin' for ya, and hope you enjoyed the picture.'
>
> 'Yeah, and we hope you'll keep coming to see us, because we like seeing you.'"

The last film starring Martin and Lewis was *Hollywood or Bust* (1956), a film that features a heavy autobiographical subtext. Martin and Lewis star as Steve and Malcolm, who each win the same car, Malcolm legitimately and Steve via a fake ticket. It is decided that they will share the winning car, but they have conflicting agendas over what they should do with it. Eventually, they drive to Hollywood at Malcolm's behest, where he endeavors to meet Anita Ekberg (and eventually does.) *Hollywood or Bust* characterized the majority of their earlier films, and the two characters travel to Hollywood the same way Martin and Lewis traveled to Hollywood together.

Nonetheless, by this point, it was too late to turn back. By the time they finished shooting *Hollywood or Bust*, their relationship was so strained that they never spoke to each other off camera. Lewis was so upset about the situation that he claimed he never bothered watching *Hollywood or Bust*.

Ironically, just as one major part of his life was ending, another part of Lewis' life was beginning. During the summer of 1956, Martin and Lewis appeared in their final televised event together, a 21 hour telethon to raise money for what was a little known disease called muscular dystrophy. This would be beginning of decades of work Lewis did on behalf of muscular dystrophy, to the point that his name would become synonymous with muscular dystrophy telethons each year.

In writing of their last performance at the Copacabana on July 24, 1956, exactly one decade after their first performance together, Lewis was painfully philosophical: "I walked out into the hallway and thought my heart would break. I was losing my best friend and I didn't know why. And if I had known why, would that have made a difference? I now think that since it had to happen, at least it happened quickly. When husbands and wives break up, it can take years, or they stay together for all the wrong reasons. Dean and I knew we had to get on with our lives, and being a team no longer worked. As sentimental as it sounds, we both had the hand of God on us until even He said, 'Enough.'" Lewis also noted the coincidental timing of the release of *Pardners* and its famous closing scene: "I've often wondered how movie audiences reacted to seeing that little epilogue on the day *Pardners* was released: July 25, 1956, the day after Martin and Lewis broke up."

Chapter 5: Martin Moves On

On August 19, 1948, Dean and Betty had their fourth child, Deana Martin, but once again the growing family belied the frictions between Martin and his wife. Betty grew increasingly exhausted by the constant affairs carried on by her husband (June Allyson and Rita Hayworth were among those he romanced during this period), and she was also left raising the children mostly by herself. In February of 1949, Dean told his family that he was going to leave them and asked that Betty acquiesce in granting him a divorce. At the time, he was entering into a relationship with Jeanne Bergier, an admiring fan who would frequent his performances, even on occasions in which Betty was in the audience. After Betty's refusal to grant a divorce (she still held out hope that they could reconcile their differences and salvage the marriage), Dean told her his mistress was pregnant. That compelled Betty to grant the divorce, and it was only later that she discovered Dean had fabricated the pregnancy in order to manipulate her into granting the divorce. Finally, in March of 1949, he and Betty finalized their divorce, and a few weeks later Martin began the longest-lasting of his three marriages by marrying Jeanne. Incredibly, Dean was granted custody of the children, subsidizing his ex-wife with alimony payments.

The aftermath of the divorce brought to light some of the shadier aspects of Martin's life. In particular, it has been suspected that he was aided by notorious gangster Anthony Fiato, who may have cheated Betty out of immense sums of alimony payments. Whether or not these rumors are true, they are part of the other allegations of mob connections held by Martin. Coincidentally or not, mobsters Sam Giancana and Tony Accardo may also have been affiliated with Frank Sinatra and the Rat Pack.

Over the course of the next decade, Martin's family expanded. In 1951, he and Jeanne had their first child, Dean Paul. Two years later, a second son, Ricci James, was born. Finally, in 1956, the couple added a third child, Gina Caroline. Martin quipped, "I've got seven kids. The three words you hear most around my house are 'hello,' 'goodbye,' and 'I'm pregnant." Martin was not an ideal father, and he had difficulty connecting with his children, but he maintained a constant presence in the household and his life was actually quite ordinary. In his memoir, Ricci Martin portrays his father in very normal terms, writing, "Because of the gallivanting image he had in the early movies and then later crystallized with Frank Sinatra and the Rat Pack, I think people have this image of him never being home. Instead, he tended to treat his stardom as any other 9-to-5 job. Actually, it was more like an 8-to-4 job."

Even as he grew increasingly famous due to his comedy performances with Jerry Lewis, Martin continued his singing career. In 1946, he recorded singles with Diamond, Apollo, and Embassy Records, and while the songs did not achieve any great acclaim, they did not end Martin's career as a singer either. In 1948, he and Lewis signed with Capitol Records, where they recorded a hit song, "That Certain Party."

Despite his brief stint singing alongside Lewis, Martin's singing career was predominantly as a soloist. In 1949, he experienced a major breakthrough after recording the hit song "Powder Your Face with Sunshine." The song reached number 10 on the charts, and though the lyrics never deviated far from the title, the song combined the cheery good feeling and cool suaveness that were present throughout his most famous songs. Over the following four years, he recorded over 80 sides, and in 1953, he recorded one of his most famous songs, the iconic "That's Amore". That song had been recorded for *The Caddy*, a film starring Martin and Lewis. "That's Amore" was a major milestone in his career, as it has been appropriated as a caricature of Italian culture. One of the most compelling aspects of Martin's rendition of it is the way in which he performs hyperbolically emotive lyrics in a cool, masculine manner. In 1954, Martin released his first two albums: *Dean Martin Sings* and *Swingin' Down Yonder*.

When Martin split from Lewis, there was little doubt that he would continue to remain popular, but the public wanted to see if his persona would change. He had long been seen as a crooning straight man to Lewis's zaniness, but he possessed the good looks and an athletic frame that lent itself to all kinds of film roles. Martin also wanted to be viewed as a more serious actor.

Martin's first film without Lewis was *Ten Thousand Bedrooms* (1957). He played a wealthy hotel owner who abuses his staff, but eventually he falls in love and the film ends (as most Hollywood films of the time do) with a successful romance. Interestingly, the film was both prophetic with regard to his late career but also wildly unsuccessful. In his review of the film, *The New York Times* critic Bosley Crowther had difficulty accepting Martin without his former comedic collaborator, noting that he was "just another nice-looking crooner without his comedy pal. Together, the two made a mutually compatible team. Apart, Mr. Martin is a fellow with little humor and a modicum of charm." This sentiment reflects the way in which *Ten Thousand Bedrooms* was likely not the proper film for Martin to appear in while attempting to extricate himself from his professional marriage with his former co-star. In particular, the film veered too close to the brand of over-the-top comedy that had characterized his earlier films. Martin retained the charm of his earlier roles and displayed the ability to play a romantic lead, but the script was comedic and he lacked a rowdy character that would contrast with his detached, calm demeanor. It likely would have been more opportune for Martin to appear in a more serious film that would have allowed viewers to observe him in an entirely fresh light.

Fortunately for Martin, his next films were the perfect antidotes to the harsh reviews that his last film received. Martin's next film was *The Young Lions* (1958), a film that is largely forgotten today but performed an invaluable function in resurrecting his career. In the film, he played the role of Michael Whiteacre, a cowardly man who grows more courageous over the course of the narrative. The film is very much a product of the 1950s. First, the running time was an epic 167 minutes, far longer than the relatively brief Martin and Lewis films. The lengthiness also reflected Hollywood's emphasis on lengthy epics, which was a response to the industry's need to distinguish itself from the increasingly severe threat of television. Finally, it is also significant that the film was directed by Edward Dmytryk, an extreme-left director with strong Popular Front connections. While the film is not particularly overt in its political affiliations, it was significant that Martin agreed to appear in a film directed by such a political maverick.

Martin's public image also benefitted from his co-stars in *The Young Lions*, Montgomery Clift and Marlon Brando. Although Brando had lost a degree of his luster with the emergence (and then death) of James Dean, he was still an enormous star within the industry, and appearing alongside him was a tremendous boost of credibility for a struggling Martin. Meanwhile, Montgomery Clift's image was less secure than Brando's. Just two years before, he had been involved in a disastrous car accident that left him with facial wounds. However, there was no doubting his acting presence, and he and Brando both epitomized the Method acting style that had been popularized during the previous decade by Lee Strasberg at the Actors Studio. The Method approach, which borrowed heavily from Stravinsky, emphasized an emotive approach in which the actor displays no personal trademarks but instead absorbs themselves completely into their role. It is easy to see how Martin would have been attracted to this approach, especially at a time when he was faced with the challenging task of disassociating himself from Lewis. Appearing in a war drama with Method actors was about as far removed as he could get from his earlier films, and it exposed viewers to a versatility they didn't know Martin possessed.

Montgomery Clift

Marlon Brando

Martin's image also evolved through his association with the Rat Pack, a group of Las Vegas entertainers who promoted an image of easy living and hedonistic consumption. Always a fun-loving man who had enjoyed gambling and alcohol, Martin was a natural fit with the fun-loving group, joining entertainment luminaries Frank Sinatra, Peter Lawford, Sammy Davis, Jr., Joey Bishop, Angie Dickinson, and Shirley MacLaine. Martin made light of his image as a laid-back but smooth womanizer who was always half in the bag, joking, "I drink because my body craves, needs alcohol. I don't drink, my body's a drunk." He also had no problem cracking wise about his own friends, saying of Shirley MacLaine, "Shirley, I love her, but her oars aren't touching the water these days."

Martin effectively swapped his association with the infantile Jerry Lewis for a more glamorous affiliation with members of the entertainment elite. He began performing at the Sands nightclub, where he held an ownership stake, and after befriending Sinatra and the other members of the group, Martin also became more political. For example, he barnstormed for John F. Kennedy in the 1960 presidential election.

Considering the new look to the Martin image offered by *The Young Lions*, it is perhaps surprising that his next film was far different than that war film. Released in 1958, Martin appeared in *Some Came Running*, directed by acclaimed Hollywood director Vincente Minnelli. The film stars Frank Sinatra as an alcoholic writer who has returned from the army, while Martin appears as his fun-loving friend, an alcoholic named Bama. Martin's role is relatively insignificant compared to Sinatra's part, but it established the precedent for most of his later film appearances. Martin was a natural as a hedonistic, pleasure-seeking individual, but *Some Came Running* is memorable mainly for Sinatra's bravura performance as a veteran struggling to integrate back into society following his time in the service. Nevertheless, Martin's later performances would borrow heavily from his appearance in that film.

Building on the acclaim of his past two films, Martin next appeared in *Rio Bravo* (1959), the film that is generally regarded as the most acclaimed of his career. It also gave him the opportunity to work with Howard Hawks, whose playful energy worked well with Martin. *Rio Bravo* built on the trend toward revising old genres. *Rio Bravo* is one of the most famous Westerns, but at the same time it veers away from the kind of classic Westerns directed by John Ford and even Hawks himself earlier in his career. The basic plot involves an eclectic community attempting to ward off a vengeful man attempting to free his brother from imprisonment.

Martin in *Rio Bravo*

On the surface, *Rio Bravo* appears very much a stereotypical Hollywood Western. Not only does it star John Wayne (rivaled only by Clint Eastwood as an icon of the genre), but the nearly 2 ½ hour running time was right up there with the epics of the decade. Additionally, the revenge-driven good guy vs. bad guy plot is central to most Westerns. However, despite its length, the film could not be further removed from the orthodox Western. While most films in the genre contain action-packed plots and dramatic views of wide vistas (John Ford's beloved Monument Valley being the archetypal example), *Rio Bravo* contains very little plot activity. The narrative plods along at a protracted pace, to the point that boredom becomes one of the principal motifs of the film. The people defending the town (the "good guys") could not be more dissimilar, and as the narrative progresses they learn to adopt a collectivist stance that eventually defeats the opposition. The apparent incongruity of John Wayne, Ricky Nelson, Dean Martin, Walter Brennan, and Angie Dickinson starring alongside one another also becomes resolved as they learn to appreciate and make use of their stark differences, culminating in a bizarre "team effort" shootout at the conclusion.

Beyond its basic plot, one of the more compelling aspects of *Rio Bravo* is the biographical resonance that surrounds each of the main characters. Martin plays an alcoholic named Dude (nicknamed Borrachon due to his drinking habit), who previously served as sheriff's deputy to Chance (played by John Wayne.) At the start of the film, Dude's alcoholism leaves him in a pathetic state, not only unable to defend his town but also himself. Over the course of the film, he achieves sobriety and reacquires his pinpoint shooting accuracy and broader sense of dignity. John Wayne's character is also in keeping with his star image, as he must overcome his trademark individualism and learn to cooperate with others. By the late 1950s, Martin had become widely viewed as a functioning alcoholic committed more to his easygoing lifestyle than any sense of professional or familial obligation, and his character in *Rio Bravo* effectively combats this image. Casting Martin as an alcoholic was hardly unusual, as he had just portrayed one in *Some Came Running*, and he would continue to be cast as one in later films, but this film frames Martin's public persona in a tragic light. Dude (Borrachon) is not the suave, tipsy figure who appears in *Some Came Running* but is instead depicted as a sad individual whose alcoholism hinders his marksmanship and worth. The narrative is one of redemption, prompting Robin Wood to state, "*Rio Bravo* remains, beyond politics, as a (political?) argument as to why we should all go on living and fighting."

In the wake of *Rio Bravo*, Martin worked with Minnelli once again, appearing alongside Judy Holliday in the film adaptation of the Broadway hit *Bells are Ringing* (1960). Considering his singing talents, it is surprising that Martin was not cast in more musicals during his career, but he rarely appeared in MGM films, the studio known for its musicals. Besides, MGM already had a stable roster of musical actors at their disposal.

After *Bells are Ringing*, Martin strengthened his affiliation with the Rat Pack, appearing in *Ocean's Eleven* (1961) and *Robin and the Seven Hoods* (1964). Of the two films, *Ocean's Eleven* has had a significantly greater impact, inspiring a host of Hollywood sequels decades later. Directed by Lewis Milestone, the film features the Rat Pack involved in a major series of heists robbing five Las Vegas casinos. The film appears almost antithetical to *Rio Bravo*, and this is true to an extent. While it should be noted that *Ocean's Eleven* is similar to the earlier film because it has Martin essentially playing himself, *Rio Brava* casts a negative light on his lifestyle while *Ocean's Eleven* glamorizes the easy-living of the Rat Pack.

Martin's image as a leisurely, hard-drinking entertainer ensured that he stayed famous, but it also had the negative effect of limiting the range of characters he was given in films. His image as a middle-aged slacker who enjoys having a good time did give him a certain niche, but that niche did not lend itself to the hardworking ethos of the male star. Ultimately, Martin had the handsome physical appearance of a leading actor, but his image was antithetical to the hard-working, progress-driven ethos of most films. As a result, he continued to appear in films in which he essentially portrayed himself. In 1964, he acted in *Kiss Me Stupid*, directed by the famous Billy Wilder. The biographical bent of his character is unmistakable, as Martin portrays a pleasure-loving crooner named Dino. Martin did not diversify his acting range, but he solidified this character type to the point that it essentially became a brand.

In the mid-1960s, Martin became even more active with his singing career and actually achieved greater popularity than he had during his early career. 1964 was a particularly successful year with the release of three of Martin's most famous songs: "Everybody Loves Somebody," "The Door is Still Open to My Heart," and "You're Nobody Till Somebody Loves You." All three songs reached number one on the Adult Contemporary charts, while "Everybody Loves Somebody," reached number one overall. Listening to the songs, there is no significant difference in singing style from his earlier songs; in fact, "Everybody Loves Somebody" was written in 1947. It's puzzling that Martin's career as a singer did better after several decades, but it was a result of the man's reputation himself instead of any change in style. At a time in which popular music had gravitated toward folk music, and with the British Invasion already underway, Martin offered a throwback to an earlier period, and a seemingly more American one at that. What is remarkable about Martin is that by the 1960s, crooning had already become antiquated, and yet he was able to gain in popularity even while singing an outmoded style of music. No matter the circumstances, Martin's brand of "cool" never went out of style. Even while Rat Pack cohort Frank Sinatra modified his style in the 1960s, Martin continued along the same path unscathed.

Chapter 6: Jerry Lewis: Actor, Writer, Producer, Director

"I was approaching thirty. I wanted to grow as a comedian, as an actor. I had, as Shakespeare said, immortal longings in me. Was Chaplin my idol? You bet your ass he was! If you're going to aim for the stars, why not pick the best? And the one thing that Charlie had—in spades—was something I'd barely tapped into: pathos." – Jerry Lewis

At first, it seemed that Lewis might not be able to continue professionally without Martin. He later remembered, "I felt incredibly alone and desperate. The fact that everyone around me seemed sure that I'd land on my feet made things worse. I didn't know what…I was going to do." But while his split with Martin was painful on both a professional and personal level, Lewis had plenty of things going in his favor outside of work. For one thing, he started staying home more in the evenings and traveling less, and he and his wife were blessed with three more children over the next four years. Scott Anthony Lewis was born on February 22, 1956, Christopher Joseph arrived in October 1957, and Anthony Joseph was born in October 1959. Though they thought five sons would be their limit, Patti later gave birth to Joseph Christopher in January 1964.

Hoping to get a little perspective, Lewis took a vacation, and just before he left to return home, he was asked to substitute for Judy Garland at a Las Vegas show. He performed her closing number, "Rock a By Your Baby with a Dixie Melody." The audience applauded wildly, so he decided to release the song as a single, with "It All Depends on You" on the flip side, in 1958. This would be the first of several records he would make over the next decade.

At the same time, despite his split with Martin, Lewis chose to stick to what he knew by staying on with Paramount. In 1956, he began working on his first solo picture, *The Delicate*

Delinquent, which was not only his first movie without Martin but also the first movie he ever produced on his own. He also co-wrote the story of a janitor accused of being a gangster and persuaded his friend Frank Tashlin to direct. Though he was now 30 years old, Lewis' character was still considered a "juvenile delinquent", and while the movie had plenty of the pathos Lewis was hoping to tap into, it did not impress the critics. One wrote:

> "If there appears in this presentment a certain sobriety that was not a detectable feature in the old Dean Martin-Jerry Lewis films, it may be respectfully acknowledged as a purpose of the new Mr. Lewis. But it also must be discovered as the cause of an unevenness in this film. Mr. Lewis, as the star of his own picture, runs a gamut from Hamlet to clown.
>
> Mr. Lewis warding off a judo wrestler or trying to fit odd-shaped blocks into odd-shaped holes is a delirious comedian. Mr. Lewis trying hard to act a man…is a mite incredible and absurd. The good intention of his message may be missed in this eccentricity.
>
> This is the trouble with the picture, written and directed by Don McGuire. It fails to concentrate the actor's comic talents. It lacks consistency. Mr. Lewis is not yet a Charlie Chaplin, though he may aim to be."

In 1958, Paramount released *Rock-A-Bye Baby*. This film was truly a family affair, with both Lewis' son Gary and his father Danny playing characters (though the latter's role ended up on the cutting room floor). Lewis also recorded several songs in for the film. Though his voice lacked the deep bass that Martin had, audiences still enjoyed hearing him, even if critics were unimpressed: "Mr. Lewis has abandoned whatever striving for maturity and subtlety he may have had. Under Frank Tashlin's direction, he and all the others in this film…are simply average slapstick buffoons. They set a tone that, despite some songs and color, makes this a very average farce."

His final film for Paramount was *The Geisha Boy*, also released in 1958. It was another Tashlin-Lewis project and pays an interesting homage to *The Bridge on the River Kwai,* in which Lewis' co-star, Sessue Hayakawa, also starred. Hayakawa's character is seen building a bridge in his backyard and whistling the familiar Colonel Bogey March, and when Lewis asks him about the bridge, he comments, "I was building bridges long before he was," after which a clip of Alec Guinness flashed across the screen.

In 1959, Lewis formally split with Paramount and formed his own company, Jerry Lewis Productions, but Paramount immediately contracted with the new company to make movies. The terms of this contract were generous; not only did Paramount pay Lewis $10 million dollars to make 14 films for them over the next 7 years, they also promised him 60% of the net profits of the pictures.

By 1960, Lewis was thoroughly tired of working with Hall Wallis and was excited to be at the end of their contract. Fittingly, his last picture with Wallis, *Visit to a Small Planet*, proved to be one spoof too many and did not impress the critics, with *The New York Times* observing, "Gore Vidal's original comedy-fantasy struck this viewer as fairly contrived stuff, cleverly turned on one obvious, running gag. Yet the idea held just enough wit and imagination to forge, for once, a Lewis frolic that might have been different. It isn't. For Mr. Lewis, Paramount, producer Hal Wallis, the two scenarists and a dutiful little cast are taking no chances of offending with something original."

Lewis next began work on *Cinderfella*, a humorous, off-beat take on the classic *Cinderella*. He began work on it in the fall of 1959 and used an extra 16 mm camera on set so that he could look at each take immediately. This paid off in some interesting ways. For example, in reviewing the film of his entrance to the ball, he noticed that his pants moved around in a way that distracted from his face, so to fix this, he pulled out a trick he had learned as a dancer and had the costume department sew elastic loops that could go under his shoes on to his pants legs. This kept them straight, no matter how he moved.

Studio shot of Lewis and Anna Maria Alberghetti in *Cinderfella*.

Unfortunately, the ball itself almost proved his undoing. After running up the very long staircase at the end of the night, he collapsed at the top with severe chest pains, the result of a mild heart attack. He spent the next four days in the hospital and two weeks resting at home, and as a result, by the time he finally did finish the movie, it was too late to release it for Christmas 1959. Believing that *Cinderfella* was at its heart a holiday movie, he insisted that he be held back and released the following year. Paramount agreed, but only if he would make another picture for them to release in the interim.

Initially, this seemed like it might be a problem because Lewis was already committed to perform that winter at the famed Fontainebleau Hotel in Miami Beach, but Lewis turned the situation to his advantage by making *The Bellboy*, a story Lewis dreamed up himself. Filmed at the Fontainebleau on a tight budget and tighter schedule, Lewis starred in and directed the picture during the day, performed on stage at night, and wrote and rewrote the script in his spare time. Fortunately, Lewis had help in the form of Bill Richmond, an old hand at staging the type of pratfalls and gags that Lewis was famous for. Lewis also got helpful suggestions from Hollywood legend Stan Laurel, and so grateful was he for Laurel's input that he named his own character Stanley in the actor's honor. Lewis also wrote a Stan Laurel character into the script, though he was portrayed by Richmond.

When Paramount refused to fund the picture, Lewis put up almost a million dollars of his own money to make the movie, and his method of reviewing each scene immediately after it was shot enabled him to finish the film in just one month, and according to one movie historian, "the movie is full of interior shots that showcase the hotel's old school elegance steeped in '50s and '60s glamour. We're talking pure Rat Pack. *The Bellboy* treats us to a visual tour as Lewis spazzes around its chic design. It's a great movie to see if you want a glimpse of Miami Beach before it was invaded by the Armani Exchange and Mansion."

The movie won Lewis a Golden Light Technical Achievement Award for his filming method, now known as video assist, but the critics were far less enthused, and one of them referenced Lewis' hopes to be another Chaplin: "If the public is still unwilling to accept Jerry Lewis as a latter-day Charlie Chaplin, it is not because the comedian hasn't tried. (…) That this attempt to mimic the master proves fruitless is only to be expected. Mr. Lewis is a frenetic performer, but he lacks a point of view. At one moment he appears an innocent victim of twentieth-century mechanization…. In the next scene, aided by camera trickery, he has become the master of his environment…. Substituting energy for insight, he is as impersonal as the mechanized society he attempts to caricature—a rubber-limbed robot making faces in a void."

Making matters worse, when *Cinderfella* was released, critics criticized both the film and Lewis, with one observing, "We'll bet good money that even the kids will be bored stiff. The gags are stale, the pacing is pure molasses and the camera glues to Mr. Lewis' feeble prancing with royal fascination. (…) …the star opens clattering doors, mashes unlighted cigarettes, drops the salt shaker in his soup—need we go on? (…) Mr. Lewis, sounding like a parched parrot, croaks three tunes. He's also the producer and believe us, no one should doubt it."

Lewis went on to write, direct and produce *The Ladies Man* and *The Errand Boy* in 1961, but he didn't act in either of those. The next movie he actually appeared in was *It's Only Money* (1962), which was directed by Frank Tashlin. He went on to wear four hats again in *The Patsy* (1964), which was originally intended to be a sequel to *The Bellboy* and even featured many similar pantomimes.

Despite his workload, it seemed that Lewis' career had passed its peak, but for his part, Lewis ignored critics. As he put it, "People think I'm against critics because they are negative to my work. That's not what bothers me. What bothers me is they didn't see the work. I have seen critics print stuff about stuff I cut out of the film before we ran it. So don't tell me about critics." He also once noted, "I've had the greatest respect for my work in this country by Americans. Critics have no brains."

Chapter 7: The Nutty Actor

"To my absolute astonishment, one pill made me feel like a human being again. The pain that had affected every waking moment, every interaction, suddenly receded, restoring my smile and leaving me free to think about all the things people normally think about." – Jerry Lewis

Since splitting with Martin several years earlier, Lewis hadn't had a big hit, but one finally came with *The Nutty Professor* (1963). In a modern retelling of the Dr. Jekyll and Mr. Hyde story, Lewis stars as a hapless professor who discovers a potion that makes him attractive to women, a similar character to the one he had played earlier in *Rock-A-Bye Baby*. People often speculated that the professor's alter ego, Buddy Love, was intended to be a sarcastic slap at Dean Martin, who was known for his suave ways with women, but Lewis always denied these claims and insisted that Buddy Love was just the classic obnoxious know-it-all that everyone runs into from time to time. He once mentioned that he wished he had made Love even more evil, since he was trying to portray the type of good versus evil struggle that exists in every person.

Regardless, critics praised the picture, with one raving, "Credit the effervescent Mr. Lewis for trying something different—a comical character study, with an edge of pathos. The surprising, rather disturbing result is less of a showcase for a clown than the revelation (and not for the first time) of a superb actor. That's why his 'Nutty Professor' may leave a lot of people thinking and hoping for more such experiments. Attaboy, Jerry."

The Nutty Professor remains Lewis' most famous film, and the one with which he is still most associated. The animated series *The Simpsons* has a character, Professor Frink, who is based on Lewis' Professor Kelp, and Lewis even made a guest appearance on the show as Frink's father. Lewis also starred in an animated version of the movie released on DVD in 2008. Comedic genius Eddie Murphy remade the movie in 1996 and then followed it up a few years later with a sequel, something Lewis had always dreamed of doing. Finally, the Tennessee Performing Arts Center in Nashville ran a musical version of the story in the summer of 2012, and Lewis himself directed the production.

1963 also saw the release of *Who's Minding the Store?,* again starring Lewis and directed by Tashlin. Lewis did not return to the director's chair until late 1964, when he began work on *The Family Jewels*. Lewis also wrote the script and produced this movie, which centers on a wealthy little girl trying to choose between the guardianship of six uncles, all played by Lewis. In fact, Lewis drew on his previous roles in *3 Ring Circus* and *The Nutty Professor* to create two of the characters. He also gave his own son and his band, Gary Lewis & The Playboys, a cameo in the movie to promote their new song, "This Diamond Ring." At least one critic didn't think Lewis' attempt to play so many roles worked: "In 'The Family Jewels,' Jerry Lewis strings together and performs seven roles, and a good, honest jeweler's appraisal is that there isn't a gem in the lot."

By this time, Lewis' popularity at Paramount was waning, and his next picture for the company, *Boeing, Boeing*, would be the last he made under his contract. When that studio chose not to renew his contract, he turned his attention to making movies for Columbia Pictures. Around the same time, Lewis suffered an injury that would change the course of his life. While guest starring on the *Andy Williams Show* in 1965, he slipped on a wet spot on stage and suffered a terrible fall that fractured his skull and chipped his spinal column. The resulting pain, dizziness and nausea were unbearable once scar tissue knotted around his spine, and the only relief he found was via a narcotic called Percodan. While one relieved most of his pain, two relieved it all, but three made him feel on top of the world. He would take three, but when that was no longer enough, he took four or five, and eventually, he was completely addicted. Of course, he didn't see it as an addiction, because in the late '60s, painkillers were considered wonder drugs and often handed out by doctors like candy. Since doctors were prescribing the pills, Lewis figured they were alright, and he kept on taking more and more as the years went on.

Lewis also went on making movies, though none would be the kind of big hit he had seen in the past. He directed and produced the terrible *Three on a Couch* and appeared in the equally bad *Way...Way Out* in 1966. *The Big Mouth*, which Lewis directed and produced in 1967, did a little bit better, as did *Hook, Line and Sinker*, his last picture for Columbia. Lewis made his final picture before a decade long hiatus in 1970: *Which Way to the Front.*

However, as his movie career declined, Lewis found more and more work on television, beginning with *The Jerry Lewis Show*, a comedic variety show that aired on ABC for two hours each Saturday evening. The show began airing in the fall of 1963, but it lasted just 13 episodes. His next variety show, which aired on NBC for two seasons in the last 1960s, was more popular, and he also continued to be a popular guest star on many different shows during this era.

Jerry Lewis on *The Jerry Lewis Show* in 1963.

Lewis filling in as host for Johnny Carson on *The Tonight Show*.

Drawing on his experience both in front of and behind the camera, Lewis began teaching a course at the University of Southern California to aspiring film directors. One of his particularly gifted students made a short film called *Amblin'* in 1968, and when Lewis saw this picture, he began showing it to his students, exclaiming, "That's what filmmaking is all about." The student's name was Steven Spielberg, and he and another of Lewis' students, George Lucas, would go on to make too many classic movies to count.

In 1972, Lewis embarked on what would be his most controversial and infamous role, which came about after he was approached by Nathan Wachsberger, a producer with an unusual script. Wachsberger asked Lewis to play the role of a washed-up clown who is recruited by the Nazis to work in a death camp to lead Jewish children into the gas chambers. At first, Lewis refused to consider the role, later writing, "The thought of playing Helmut still scared the hell out of me". Instead, he suggested, "Why don't you try to get Sir Laurence Olivier? I mean, he doesn't find it too difficult to choke to death playing Hamlet. My bag is comedy, Mr. Wachsberger, and you're asking me if I'm prepared to deliver helpless kids into a gas chamber? Ho-ho. Some laugh — how do I pull it off?"

However, after reconsidering the script, Lewis decided to try his hand at the role. By this time, his career in comedy was pretty much over, and he may have thought he could make a new start as a dramatic actor. Either way, in February 1972 he traveled to Germany and visited Auschwitz and Dachau, also filming some exterior shots for the picture. He even began starving himself to look more like a concentration camp victim, losing 35 pounds off his already thin frame. All the while, the same drugs that were keeping him out of pain and free from hunger were influencing his personality, and those working with him on set later described him as "distracted, nervous and preoccupied with money". He and Wachsberger often argued over details of the film's release and nearly ended up in court over production costs and financing.

While the film was never publically released, it left a lasting impression on the few that saw it post-production. Actor Harry Shearer observed, "With most of these kinds of things, you find that the anticipation, or the concept, is better than the thing itself. But seeing this film was really awe-inspiring, in that you are rarely in the presence of a perfect object. This was a perfect object. This movie is so drastically wrong, its pathos and its comedy are so wildly misplaced, that you could not, in your fantasy of what it might be like, improve on what it really is. 'Oh My God!' — that's all you can say." Shearer added that watching it was like "if you flew down to Tijuana and suddenly saw a painting on black velvet of Auschwitz. You'd just think 'My God, wait a minute! It's not funny, and it's not good, and somebody's trying too hard in the wrong direction to convey this strongly-held feeling.'"

Some criticized Lewis for making Helmut too sympathetic, a la the famous Ringling Bros. clown Emmett Kelly, rather than the evil man the role originally called for. For his part, Lewis maintains, "You will never see it. No one will ever see it, because I am embarrassed at the poor work." On another occasion he admitted, "...in terms of that film I was embarrassed. I was ashamed of the work, and I was grateful that I had the power to contain it all, and never let anyone see it. It was bad, bad, bad." However, his museum tells a different story, saying, "The film has been tied up in litigation ever since, and all of the parties involved have never been able to reach an agreeable settlement. Jerry hopes to someday complete the film, which remains to this day a significant expression of cinematic art, suspended in the abyss of international litigation".

The early 1970s were a particularly difficult time for Lewis personally as well. Frank Tashlin, a friend and mentor of sorts, died in 1972, and his father suffered a serious stroke the same year.

On top of that, his oldest son Gary, once the carefree leader of a '60s style rock band, had been drafted and shipped off to Vietnam, and when he returned he brought with him baggage that neither Lewis nor many other Americans were prepared to deal with. Professionally, he was unable to get any sort of interest in the type of cheerful family films he enjoyed making, as the 1960s had spawned a generation of young people who preferred sex, drugs and rock-and-roll to bumbling stooges.

Meanwhile, the pills that were supposed to make everything better continued making things worse. He was now taking 6 high powered Percodans a day and was beginning to suffer severe physical and mental side effects that had a serious effect on his marriage and family. Everything finally came to a head on the evening of October 2, 1973, his 29th wedding anniversary. Lewis recalled, "I locked myself into my bathroom, took a .38 pistol out of a pad-locked drawer, and stuck the barrel in my mouth. I cocked the hammer. I was ready to go. All the pain, all my troubles, would vanish. I sat there like that for what felt like forever. Then, through the door, I heard my boys, running and playing somewhere off in the house. I took the gun out of my mouth and locked it back in the drawer. I would struggle along somehow." He also noted, ""I had to get my own house in order…. My spine pain was like an insatiable monster. I was living in a private world of agony and addiction, and my family saw me—when they saw me—at my worst. I kept those who had been nearest to me at the greatest distance, and some permanent emotional scars formed. My long-suffering wife suffered the most. My boys came a close second."

Chapter 8: Martin's Later Years

Martin and Sinatra on *The Dean Martin Show*

Martin continued his prolific singing career from 1965-1975, often producing several songs a year, but he never achieved the popularity he had garnered earlier in the decade. Dean also continued to act in films, but he never returned to the melodramatic territory of *The Young Lions*. It's ironic that *The Young Lions* is largely responsible for resurrecting his film career, and yet he restricted himself to comedies and Westerns late in his career. In 1966, Martin starred in *The Silencers* (1966), a spy spoof that played on the popularity of the James Bond films. The film starred Martin as a retired secret agent who becomes involved in a plot concerning an atomic bomb in New Mexico. In the end, Martin's character defeats his nemesis and wins the girl. In spite of the formulaic plot, the film was a major box office success, and Martin would actually star in three loose sequels over the following four years: *Murderers' Row* (also released in 1966), *The Ambushers* (1967), and *The Wrecking Crew* (1968). None of the films were critically acclaimed, but the pace at which they were released attests to Martin's work ethic.

Late in his career, Martin starred in either Westerns, big-budget disaster films, or comedic spoofs of Westerns. In 1970, he appeared in *Airport*, the film that spawned the disaster-epic film and inspired a host of comedic variations of the subgenre. Surprisingly (given his age), Martin starred in the action-packed police drama *Mr. Ricco* in 1975, playing the role of a detective. The film borrowed from the success of *Dirty Harry* and *French Connection* (1971), although Martin was too old to properly inhabit the role. Otherwise, during the late 1960s and 1970s Martin predominantly appeared in Westerns, including *Texas Across the River* (1966), *Rough Night in Jericho* (1967), *5 Card Stud* (1968), and *Showdown* (1973). Considering that he was already past the age of 50 by the time that *Texas Across the River* was made, it is fair to wonder how he could be cast in such a rugged role. However, by the late 1960s and 1970s, the Western was aging as a genre, and casting older stars corresponded with the more middle-aged viewing demographic. Meanwhile, Western films starring younger actors, like the Spaghetti Westerns with Clint Eastwood and films like *Butch Cassidy and the Sundance Kid*, were revisionist Westerns geared toward a younger audience.

Although Martin continued to find steady employment as a singer and movie star, his most significant occupation during the late 1960s and early 1970s was as a television host. In 1965, *The Dean Martin Show* debuted, naturally featuring Martin as the show's host. On the show, Martin entertained stars and perfected his image as a half-drunk, middle-age playboy. During each show, he performed two musical numbers, one serious and the other more comedic, thereby fulfilling his most famous functions as a comedy actor and romantic crooner.

The show also gained publicity (and notoriety) for Martin's behavior, which occasionally probed the limits of risqué conduct. He routinely flirted with his female guests, offering quips that were loaded with sexual innuendo. Another signature of the show was the half-drunken glass of whiskey that was constantly at his side. Although it has been popularly alleged that the glass was often filled with apple juice, it served as a prop that reinforced the easy-living Las Vegas lifestyle of the Rat Pack. *The Dean Martin Show* was an immediate success, and in 1967 Martin signed a record contract with NBC that gave him $34 million over three years.

Martin and guest Florence Henderson on *The Dean Martin Show*

At a time in which television was gaining in popularity, *The Dean Martin Show* was able to distance itself from the competition by banking on Martin's star power. There were other popular shows, but Martin was the first singer and actor who seamlessly transitioned into television, and the opportunity to watch Martin perform two songs during each show was a major competitive advantage for the show, at least until Martin's charm began to wear away. In the early 1970s, the show declined in popularity as audiences grew tired of Martin's dated playboy image. One review from 1972 noted, "When was it that Dean Martin ceased to be in any way amusing?...the humor had been distilled from the sweat socks of junior high school hoodlets. The whole thing reminded me of acne." This review also reflected the influence of feminism and cultural studies, which had just begun to emerge. Martin's playboy act was suddenly deemed sexist and offensive, and the show was ended in 1974.

With the termination of *The Dean Martin Show*, Martin began to remake his image, shifting away from musical performances and more toward comedy. In 1974, he began a new show for NBC titled *The Dean Martin Celebrity Roast*. As with *The Dean Martin Show*, the episodes were predicated on a celebrity guest, but unlike the former show, Martin would "roast" the guest. The show was a hit and lasted until 1984. At a time in which he was scaling down in his film appearances and musical performances, *The Dean Martin Celebrity Roast* kept Martin in the public sphere. It also helped solidify his reputation in every respect, as the charming host roasted all kinds of individuals. Perhaps most ironically, given that he wasn't writing his own material, Martin once joked about Bob Hope, "As a young boy, Bob didn't have much to say. He couldn't afford writers then."

One of the more significant developments for Martin during the 1970s was his divorce from Jeanne, to whom he had been married for over 20 years. After filing for divorce, an unusual move for a husband, Martin joked, "I know it's the gentlemanly thing to let the wife file. But, then, everybody knows I'm no gentleman." In 1973, he married Catherine Hawn, a woman young enough to be his daughter. He was deeply committed to her at first and adopted her daughter Sasha, but the age gap between the two eventually rendered the marriage untenable. They divorced after three years.

By the turn of the 1980s, Martin entertainment career was concentrated almost exclusively on his show. He did appear in two over-the-top comedies, *The Cannonball Run* (1981) and *Cannonball Run II* (1984), but his film appearances were infrequent. Finally, after a run of roughly 10 years, *The Dean Martin Celebrity Roast* ended in 1984. Although Martin did not formally announce his retirement, he effectively retired when his show ended. The rest of his life would revolve around golf and leisure.

Martin with Sammy Davis, Jr., Shirley MacLaine, and Sinatra on the Set of *Cannonball*

Run II

After the close of his show in 1984, Martin began a reclusive lifestyle that could not have been more different than the very public image of him as a glamorous Rat Pack icon. The public perception of Martin as an outgoing man was always largely inaccurate, but Martin became even more withdrawn in his later years. He enjoyed golfing and held memberships at the Bel Air and Riviera Country Clubs in California, but he otherwise spent the bulk of his time at home watching television. He rarely saw even his closest friends, and the man known for being a quintessential drinker hated to host parties or attend them.

By this point, Martin was rich, but he also made a series of wise real estate investments that added to his wealth and guaranteed his financial stability. On occasion, he performed in public, most notably when he appeared on a CBS Telethon with Jerry Lewis in 1976 at the behest of Sinatra. That brought about a public reconciliation with his former co-star. In the early 1980s, the Rat Pack went on a reunion tour, but Martin clashed with Sinatra and the tour was not a success. His final shows were in 1989-1990 in Las Vegas.

Martin's reclusive nature surprised many, but he had always been more subdued than Jerry Lewis, Frank Sinatra, and his other show business partners. His wife Jeanne once noted, "No one, nothing impressed him deeply." Beneath his façade as an entertainer, Martin was a very simple man. While he enjoyed his liquor and was adept at promoting his image as a functioning alcoholic, he thrived on routine, and his prolific careers in singing, film and television show that he was truly a dedicated and hard worker.

The final decade of Martin's life was relatively somber. In March of 1987, his son Dean died in a fighter plane crash over the San Bernardino Mountains. Lewis attended the funeral anonymously, but Martin learned that he had been there and called him a few days later. Lewis wrote, "We talked for an hour. He cried, I cried. I said, 'Life's too short, my friend. This is one of those things that God hands us, and we have to somehow go on with our lives. That's what Dino would have wanted.' I was trying to get him to see that one had to find a way to go forward."

The two men would appear on stage once more and for the last time on June 2, 1989, Martin's 72nd birthday. Lewis surprised him with a birthday cake during a performance and Martin told him quite audibly, "I love you and I mean it." Lewis replied, "Here's to seventy-two years of joy you've given the world. Why we broke up, I'll never know."

Nevertheless, Martin was never able to shake off the lingering depression over his son's death, and he became even more withdrawn and ventured outside his house even less (Ricci Martin). Subsequently, in 1993 Martin was diagnosed with lung cancer, and he announced his official retirement in 1995. The cancer transformed him into a skeletal figure during his final years, and he died on Christmas Day in 1995.

Analyzing Dean Martin's career can be a tough undertaking since he performed in a wide array of entertainment platforms and remained successful for such an extended period of time. At the same time, no matter the arena, Martin essentially appeared as the same figure, a laid-back Italian crooner who women fantasized over and men attempted to emulate. Thus, the central paradox of Martin's career is the manner in which it is both incredibly diverse and at the same time remarkably constant. In a sense, what differentiate Martin's films and entertainment productions from one another are not his own characters but the different actors with whom he was cast. In the Jerry Lewis films and in *The Dean Martin Show*, Martin essentially portrays the same suave, calm figure. The major difference lies in the fact that Jerry Lewis appears in one, while he occupies center stage in the other. Whether appearing alongside Jerry Lewis, Frank Sinatra, or by himself, Martin's own image remained relatively intact throughout his career.

Martin's personal life magnifies the stark contrast between his upbringing and the fame he later enjoyed. Indeed, it is almost unfathomable that a social outcast who was ridiculed for his accent and quit school altogether in the 10th grade could grow up to become such an entertainment legend. As a student and a young man, he was entirely unremarkable, and had Martin's career been unsuccessful, it is difficult to envision him achieving success in any other venue. At the same time, it is unlikely that his fame will ever disappear, and few stars are able to enjoy the wide appeal Dean Martin has had across many generations. As Bob Greene noted, "The coolness of Dean Martin seamlessly crosses generations; young guys heading for a weekend in Las Vegas with their buddies understand his appeal just as viscerally as their grandparents do."

Even if they were not always critically successful, Martin's enduring appeal ensures that his songs and films will forever remain culturally relevant.

Chapter 9: Lewis Rises from the Ashes

"I don't want to be remembered. I want the nice words when I can hear them." – Jerry Lewis

It would have been nice if all Lewis's problems had immediately cleared up after the night he contemplated suicide, but real life was nothing like his movies and he knew it. Instead of changing everything, or even anything at that time, he simply carried on as best he could, doing what little work he was offered and throwing himself heart and soul into his annual Labor Day Telethons. Though he would later confess that there were a number of events during this time in his life that he could not remember, he also wrote about the one he would never forget: "I was on stage…doing 'Telethon '76'…Frank [Sinatra]…interrupted, saying…'Hey, send my friend out here, will ya?' And out walked Dean Martin, my partner, and I was in a time warp. My hands got sweaty, my mouth turned dry. I tried to stand tall as he approached me, and we hugged hard, very hard. He kissed me on the cheek, and I did the same to him. The audience in the theater was going wild. For the first time in twenty years, we stood side by side—as always, Dean stage right, me stage left. 'I think it's about time, don't you?' Frank said. The two of us nodded yes in tandem."

Though the reconciliation was not instant, that event was a beginning, and the two would work together over the next several years to rebuild their relationship. Meanwhile, Lewis was up to 13 Percodan a day and traveling the world in search of something to relieve his pain. Ultimately, it was not until he collapsed while visiting a friend in a hospital that he finally got clean. His doctor put him under sedation while he detoxed over a 10 day period, and during the same time, Lewis also recovered from a severe stomach ulcer that had been only days from taking his life. In reference to the kind of pain he was suffering, he later noted, "If I found the cure for dystrophy tomorrow, I would do a telethon in four weeks for acute pain that in this country is a bigger problem than cancer, heart, sickle cell, anemia, name it. It is - it's hitting 70 million Americans."

Though Lewis was now free from Percodan, his problems were far from over. In 1980, he was forced to declare bankruptcy when Jerry Lewis Cinemas and National Cinema Corp. went bankrupt and closed. Still, he kept going, continuing work on his first picture in nearly a decade, *Hardly Working*. Lewis wrote and directed the picture, which was almost never completed because of his financial difficulties. Lewis also found it difficult to work in Florida, which was a trendy place to make smaller budget pictures: "...the whole experience was a mixed bag. ...I have to admit that the awful strain of the past ten years showed in every part of my work. The movie didn't really hang together, and not so surprisingly, I looked terrible in it." While making *Hardly Working*, Lewis met Sandee Pitnick, and though she was younger than two of his sons, the two began an affair that brought his 36 year marriage to Patti Palmer to an end in 1980.

Hardly Working made over $50 million, but it was not popular with critics, one of whom observed, "In the hands of another director, and working with this same material, Mr. Lewis might well seem madcap, or at least mad. But when he directs his own pratfalls, he becomes his own worst enemy. As the subordinate characters wildly overreact to Mr. Lewis's antics, he divides his energies between comedy and pathos, and winds up alternately undermining the gags or playing cutup in the 'serious' moments. The result is utter confusion."

In spite of these and similar reviews, Lewis decided to continue his comeback with *The King of Comedy*, beginning work on the film in 1981, but shortly after its European release the following year, Lewis suffered another heart attack. Since his American audience was still not as strong as his European following, the movie was not released in the United States until 1983, but the director Martin Scorsese praised Lewis and his work ethic, while Lewis spoke with humor about Scorsese's tricks to get him ready to perform. *The King oj Comedy* was both a critical and box office success and earned Lewis his first British Academy Film Award nomination for Best Actor in a Supporting Role.

Over the next decade, Lewis would continue to make occasional movies, but few of them would see theatrical release. He directed *Cracking Up* during the mid-1980s, but it was released straight to cable, and he also appeared in several European pictures, including *Slapstick (Of Another Kind)* in 1982. He remained popular in France throughout the 1980s, especially with the release of *Retenez Moi...Ou Je Fais Un Malheur* (*The Defective Detective*) and *Par où t'es rentré ? On t'a pas vu sortir (How Did You Get In? We Didn't See You Leave*).

Lewis played an uncharacteristically serious role in the ABC Made for TV Movie *Fight for Life,* starring as the father of a sick child in need of a new but as yet unapproved drug to survive. Given his long time association with the fight against muscular dystrophy, it seems likely that he made this movie primarily to draw attention to the need for a better, quicker process to approve new drugs for the treatment of life threatening illnesses.

In 1992, Lewis adopted his only daughter, Danielle Sara, in March, and that fall, he had a brief appearance on an episode of the hit TV show *Mad About You.* Two years later, he made his Broadway debut, starring as the Devil in *Damn Yankees.* Though he initially joined the cast as a replacement for another actor, he handled the part so well that he was invited to stay on with the show for the remainder of its run in the United States and London. His performance earned him a Theatre World Award.

With so many other opportunities to perform, Lewis has made fewer and fewer feature films, including appearances in *Arizona Dream* in 1994 and *Funny Bones* in 1995. But as his film career was obviously winding down and he was getting older, he was beginning to get more recognition for his entire body of work, leading to the American Comedy Awards Lifetime Achievement Award in 1997 and a Golden Lion Honorary Award in 1999.

Unfortunately, the 1990s and 2000s have also brought an increasing number of health problems his way. In 1999, Lewis contracted meningitis while appearing on a performance tour in Australia, requiring him to cancel his performances as he remained hospitalized in Darwin for over five months. On top of this, he was plagued with problems related to his health insurance, leading the Australian press to accuse him of not paying his bills. He felt that the impact on his life and career of these accusations was so severe that he sued his insurer for $100 million.

The meningitis also exacerbated Lewis' struggles with Type 1 Diabetes, as well as his heart condition. In 2000, he was prescribed Prednisone for pulmonary fibrosis, but the weight gain was so severe that he had to be weaned off of it during the fall of 2001. Thankfully, the following year, he was implanted with a Medtronic "Synergy" neurostimulator in his back, which significantly reduced the pain he had still been experiencing from his 1966 injury. When asked to explain the new gizmo, Lewis has been happy to oblige, saying, "This is the pain pacemaker. I've got a battery under my skin. From that battery are two electrodes that go into the spine where they cut bone away to accommodate it. Now I put on the power here. If I have the pain, the stimulator starts. It's tingling, like when your foot falls asleep, you know?" In fact, he is so good at explaining his new machine that he has become a spokesman for the company.

In 2006, Lewis suffered another heart attack while flying from San Diego to New York, and while he was hospitalized for treatment, doctors learned that he also had pneumonia. They placed two stents in to open up arteries, and though he had to cancel several engagements during this time, the procedure was successful and Lewis made a full recovery.

As his health has grown increasingly precarious, countries and organizations from around the world have continued to honor Lewis' life and work. In 2004, he received the Los Angeles Film Critics Association's Career Achievement Award, and the following year, the Primetime Emmy's honored him with the Governor's Award. He also received the Goldene Kamera Honorary Award from Germany, and a 2006 appearance on *Law & Order: Special Victims Unit* earned him a Satellite Award for Outstanding Guest Star.

Lewis in 2005. Picture by Patty Mooney of Crystal Pyramid Productions

One of the most significant awards Lewis has ever earned is the Légion d'honneur given to him in 2006 by the French Minister of Culture for being the "French people's favorite clown". Americans have long wondered about the love the French people have for Lewis and his movies, and likewise, the French have often expressed surprise that Lewis is not more popular back home. There was even a book written in 2001 entitled "W*hy the French Love Jerry Lewis*." Apparently, the French appreciate Lewis for the way in which he was able to perform all aspects of filmmaking, much like Howard Hawks and Alfred Hitchcock before him.

In the past few years, other awards continued to pour in. Lewis was inducted into the New Jersey Hall of Fame in 2009 and received the 2009 Jean Hersholt Humanitarian Award during the 2009 Academy Awards Ceremony. Chapman University awarded him an Honorary Doctorate of Humane Letters during the 2010 Muscular Dystrophy Association Telethon, which would prove to be the last telethon that Lewis hosted. As perspectives on the disabled have changed through the years, some people came to feel that his interaction with "his kids" was unacceptably demeaning, but Lewis still remains involved in the fight against the disease.

In 2011, Lewis won the Ellis Island Medal of Honor, awarded to first and second generation immigrants who have made significant contributions to American life and culture. He also contracted with Artificial Intelligence Entertainment and Capital Films to remake *The Bellboy*, *Cinderfella* and *The Family Jewels*. Lewis would not star in these pictures but would serve as the films' co-executive producer. That same year, Lewis produced and appeared in his own life's story, *Method to the Madness of Jerry Lewis*.

In 2009, Lewis attended the Cannes Film Festival and announced that he would be starring in *Max Rose*, his first major role since *The King of Comedy*. Two years later, he was back at Cannes to premier the movie. Cannes Film Festival directorThierry Frémaux told one journalist, "Jerry Lewis invented a singular style, uniquely staged and choreographed. In fact, when America was celebrating the showman, the comedian, France was recognizing the artist with a unique voice and eye." Hopefully, that unique voice continues to speak and that unique eye continues to twinkle for many years to come.

Bibliography

Carnes, Mark C., ed. *American National Biography: Supplement 2*. Oxford: Oxford University Press, 2005.

Crowther, Bosley. "Ten Thousand Bedrooms." *The New York Times*. 4 April 1957. Retrieved from http://movies.nytimes.com/movie/review?res=9F00E2D61E3EE63ABC4C53DFB266838C649EDE.

Cyclops. "The Witless Reign of King Leer." *Life* 7 April 1972: 14.

Greene, Bob. "Why Dean Martin's Still So Cool." *CNN*. 8 April 2012. Retrieved from http://www.cnn.com/2012/04/08/opinion/greene-dean-martin.

Lewis, Jerry, & James Kaplan. *Dean and Me: (A Love Story)*. New York: Broadway Books, 2005.

Martin, Deana, and Wendy Holden. *Memories are Made of This: Dean Martin Through His Daughter's Eyes*. New York: Three Rivers Press, 2004.

Martin, Ricci. *That's Amore: A Son Remembers His Father*. Lanham: Taylor Trade Publishing, 2002.

Smith, John L. *The Animal in Hollywood: Anthony Fiato's Life in the Mafia*. New York: Barricade Books, 1998.

Tosches, Nick. *Dino: Living High in the Dirty Business of Dreams*. New York: Dell Publishing, 1992.

Wood, Robin. *Rio Bravo*. London: BFI, 2003.

Books by Jerry Lewis

The Total Film-Maker. Random House. (1971)

Jerry Lewis: In Person. Atheneum. (1982)

Instruction Book for... "Being a Person" or (Just Feeling Better). Executive Books. (2004)

and James Kaplan. *Dean and Me: (A Love Story)*. Doubleday. (2011)

Books About Jerry Lewis

Gehman, Richard. *That Kid: The Story of Jerry Lewis*. New York: Avon Books. 1964.

Levy, Shawn Anthony. *King of Comedy: The Life and Art of Jerry Lewis*. New York: St. Martin's Press. 1997.

Marx, Arthur. *Everybody Loves Somebody Sometime (Especially Himself): The Story of Dean Martin and Jerry Lewis*. New York, NY: Hawthorn Books, 1974,

Young, Jordan R. (1999) *The Laugh Crafters: Comedy Writing in Radio & TV's Golden Age*. Beverly Hills: Past Times Publishing. 1999.

Made in United States
North Haven, CT
29 June 2022

20740949R00035